The Running of the Bulls
San Fermín

Editorial Everest would like to thank you for purchasing this book. It has been created by an extensive
and complete publishing team made up of photographers, illustrators and authors specialised in the field of tourism,
together with our modern cartography department. Everest guarantees that the contents of this work were completely
up to date at the time of going to press, and we would like to invite you to send us any information that helps us
to improve our publications, so that we may always offer
QUALITY TOURISM.

Please send your comments to:
Editorial Everest. Dpto. de Turismo
Apartado 339 – 24080 León (España)
e-mail: turismo@everest.es

everest

Editorial management: Raquel López Varela

Editorial coordination: Aizkorri argitaletxea y Mónica Santos del Hierro

Text and the Running of the Bulls Route map: Mariano Sinués del Val

Photographs:

> Archivo Carmelo Butini Echarte: pages 3, 5, 8 (above and down), 14, 18 (above), 21, 22 (above), 24, 31, 36, 37, 38, 39, 45, 58, 59, 60-61.
> Arturo (Arch. Carlos Leandro): pages 33 (down), 48, 54-55.
> Ayerra Bastero, José Ángel: pages 6, 7, 10-11, 16, 18 (down), 19, 20-21, 22 (centre and down), 23, 25 (down), 28 (above), 32.
> Cia Úriz, Julio (Arch. C. Butini): page 13.
> Eugui Gauna, César: pages 33 (above), 44, 50-51, 56-57.
> García Garrabella / Foto Chapresto: page 35.
> Lacunza Ayerra, Miguel: page 25 (above).
> Leache, José Luis: pages 26, 27 (down), 29, 30, 42, 53.
> Mena, V. (Arch. C. Butini): pages 15, 47.
> Muñoz Monllor, Fermín; pages 43, 46.
> Postales Iruña: pages 41, 64.
> Postales Vaquero (Arch. Javier Bergua, Colecc. Iruña): page 52.
> Retegui Zubieta, Javier: (Arch. C. Butini): pages 34, 40.
> Retegui Zubieta, Javier: page 28 (down).
> Sinués del Val, Mariano: pages 12 (left and right), 62 (above and down), 63.
> Urcabe (Arch. C. Butini): page 4.
> Zaragüeta Zabalo, Gerardo (Arch. C. Butini): pages 17, 27 (above).

Translation: Sheila Anne Naylor by Babyl Traducciones

Layout: Luis Alonso

Digital image processing: David Aller y Ángel Rodríguez

Street maps and road maps: © EVEREST

© EDITORIAL EVEREST, S. A.
Carretera León-La Coruña, km 5 — LEÓN
ISBN: 978-84-441-3038-5
Legal deposit: LE. 1055-2008
Printed in Spain — Impreso en España

EDITORIAL EVERGRÁFICAS, S. L.
Carretera León-La Coruña, km 5
LEÓN (España)

www.everest.es
Atención al cliente: 902 123 400

7-7-1912. Leading oxen, Gamero Cívico bulls and herdsmen covering the last few metres up to the old bullring. This particular section, along Calle Espoz y Mina (now named Duque de Ahumada) has existed until 1921. Both bulls and runners were obliged to turn right at the end of Estafeta and there wasn't the slope down to the bullring that we see today at the entrance to the callejón, the barricaded passage between the bullring and the seats.

The *Encierro* of Running of the Bulls, amounts to what was once an everyday activity being upheld as a spectacle, moving the beasts from the livestock farms to the livestock pens or corrals on the outskirts of the cities and from there on to the city centres. Bullfighting was first reported in Pamplona back in the 14th century and at the time they were held in no-man's-land between the towns or medieval districts, destined for processions, fiestas and bullfights. Plaza del Castillo, transformed from the time of the Renaissance into the city's magnificent public square, was where the bullfighting continued to be held until the 19th century. And this was where the running of the bulls finished up for the bulls from the nearby lands, having covered the terraces upon which the city was raised by making their way along streets which traced the old bed of the Santo Domingo gully, one of the historical routes into the old city. The construction of a permanent bullring in 1844 brought about a new route, which for the first time included Calle Estafeta, and the new bullring, inaugurated in 1922, is responsible for the present day route.

In this book it has been our intention to include everything which is related to, shapes, defines and is the driving force behind the Running of the Bulls, its protagonists and its great moments, its history and its developments, the excitement of the chase, how and why, in the course of these few days, at eight o clock in the morning, half the world revolves around what's going on at *Sanfermines*.

The anticipation of seeing the bulls through one of the open windows in the walls of the corrals, in this case from Domecq. A visit to the Gas Corrals is now a customary event the week before and during the Sanfermines festivities.

The running of the bulls began in 1911. Led by leading oxen and herded by herdsmen, the bulls set off from what was the entrance through the city's walls, known as the Portal de la Rochapea (a few years before it was demolished), and also the place the bulls were gathered the night before the run.

THE FOUR PHASES IN THE RUNNING OF THE BULLS
THE GAS CORRALS

Originally established in 1889 in what was once an old gas factory, but following successive reforms and improvements they were finally demolished in 2004 and new ones built alongside the old. From then on, *Calleja de los Toros*, the old alleyway and originally the first stretch of the Bull Running route, become an integrated passage amongst the corrals. The bulls always arrive in Pamplona before the fiestas, except that is for the one on the 14th, and in this case, due to the shortage of space, they arrive on the 7th. For this same reason, the spirited bulls for the bullfights against the mounted bullfighters and the young fighting bulls are led directly to the corrals at the bullring. Through glazed windows set in the walls of each corral, the people of Pamplona, bullfighting aficionados and bull-runners, have gathered for a good few years now to get a close up look at the bulls from the week before the fiestas.

THE ENCIERRILLO

The day before the actual running of the bulls, the bulls and leading oxen are led from their corrals to those of Santa Domingo where they spend the night. From 1889 up until 1929 the old Running of the Bulls also took place from the Sadar copses, like they do today. Popularly known as the *Encierrillo*, or the short Running of the Bulls, this involves four hundred metres of almost nocturnal Running of the Bulls from the Gas Corrals, by the Rochapea Bridge, dropping down to Portal Nuevo as far as the corral for the hilly Cuesta de Santo Domingo stretch. Complete with fencing. There's no fixed time, it takes place at nightfall, around ten o clock at night. After hearing the sound of a horn and in the presence of only the herdsmen, the bulls are left to wander amongst the leading oxen. The running takes place in silence and without any lights except for the street lamps. The emotion is quite distinct, almost ceremonial. There are some runners who study the behaviour of the bulls during the *encierrillo* in an attempt to calculate their possible reaction on the following day.

CORRAL DE SANTO DOMINGO

The corral is located at the foot of the *Museo de Navarra*, set on the curve which marks the start of the hilly stretch on the Cuesta de Santo Domingo. Since 1887 the bulls have spent the night before the Bull-Run in an official enclosure within the walls, inside the Rochapea bulwark. Until its demolition at the beginning of the 20th century, the running bulls passed through the *Portal de la Rochapea*, the gates which accessed the walled city. Here too the rocket was fired to announce the start of the Running of the Bulls.

2004. The magnificent sight of a jabonero *(the name refers to the shading in the bull's coat) with its spectacular horns. This bull's light and dark shaded coat highlights its muscle tone and this also serves as an example of the sort of bulls sent by the ranches to the* San Fermín *festival.*

2004. A serious look on the face and horns of these specimens as they rest in the corrals at midday.

The old Gas Corrals as they were before being demolished and reconstructed in 2004 (the new ones are more modern and convenient with more facilities but don't have quite the same charm).

Impressive and characteristic sight of the bulls from Miura, resting in the corrals awaiting Sunday's running of the bulls.

THE RUNNING OF THE BULLS

At the time, there are no details which specify at which moment the *mozos*, the bullfighter's assistants began to run in front of the bulls in Pamplona. Bullfights are documented from the 14th century.

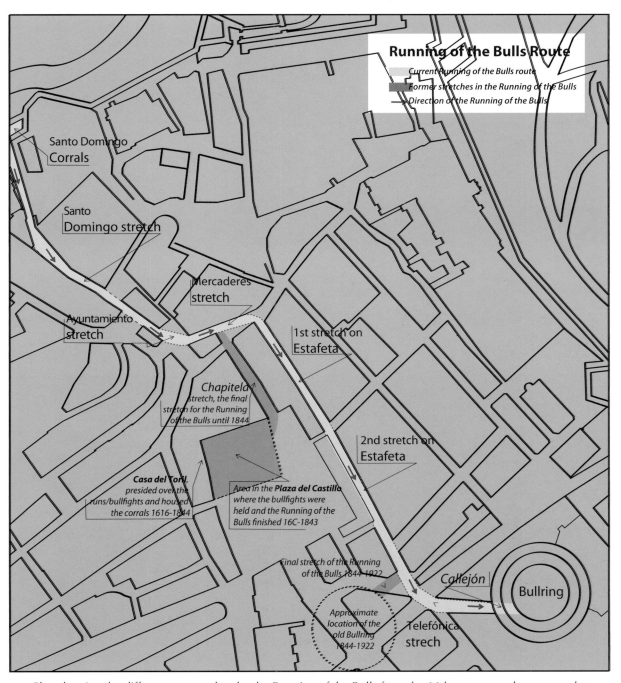

Running of the Bulls Route

Current Running of the Bulls route
Former stretches in the Running of the Bulls
Direction of the Running of the Bulls

Santo Domingo **Corrals**

Santo **Domingo stretch**

Mercaderes stretch

Ayuntamiento stretch

1st stretch on Estafeta

Chapitela stretch, the final stretch for the Running of the Bulls until 1844

2nd stretch on Estafeta

Casa del Toril, presided over the runs/bullfights and housed the corrals 1616-1844

Area in the **Plaza del Castillo** where the bullfights were held and the Running of the Bulls finished 16C-1843

Final stretch of the Running of the Bulls 1844-1922

Callejón

Bullring

Approximate location of the old Bullring 1844-1922

Telefónica strech

Plan showing the different routes taken by the Running of the Bulls from the 16th century to the present day.

The first more or less reliable news on the Running of the Bulls dates back to the beginning of the 18th century. The bulls began their running engrossed in the leading oxen. These were preceded by an expert on horseback, the justice deputy or the *Abanderado de San Fermín*. The herdsmen ran behind. The locals joined in on foot and, with their lances and pikes, helped to keep the bulls on track, until that was, these pieces of equipment were prohibited in 1738 and

Previous doble page, for the last fifty years, before running the Encierro *the* mozos *have always sung the now classic "A San Fermín pedimos…" to an image of their Patron Saint - decorated by neckerchiefs from the* Peñas *or clubs.*

Down left, image of San Fermín *set in a niche built in 1981 into a wall on the sloping street of Santo Domingo. In the past it was placed in a window in the old Military Hospital, now demolished. Signposts for the running of the bulls, placed at strategic points along the route for the benefit of the tourists (which incidentally the bulls are known not to consult during the running).*

"spontaneous" participation came to be restricted to harmless souls. The route at this time was very similar to the present day route, except that after Mercaderes it continued along Calle Chapitela. The route finished, just as it does today in Plaza del Castillo, at the door to number 37, and the site of the Casa de los Toriles corrals (1616-1844) and the once dismountable wooden bullring.

Next page, the forties. Two bulls at the head of the Encierro *as they come into the Plaza del Ayuntamiento. Until it was demolished in 1977, the way through between* Casa Seminario *– seen on the right – and the Ayuntamiento or town hall created an authentic bottleneck which made the bull running even more dangerous. The* mozos *on the left join the rest of the herd looking like they wish they were invisible.*

The thirties. Exchanged looks between bull and runner in a compromising situation, at a point of no escape in front of the old Military Hospital. Since it was demolished in the eighties the semicircular windows have disappeared, a place where more than one runner has been known to take refuge and closely watch the bulls as they pass.

By the 19th century the route was almost identical to the current one. That said, there were however two periods (1844-1855 and 1861-1867) during which the bulls entered from the opposite side of the city and covered a much shorter distance to the bullring, reducing the Running of the Bulls to almost nothing. In 1844, the official opening of the fixed bullring caused Plaza del Castillo to be abandoned and Calle Estafeta became included in the Running of the Bulls.

Next page, 9-7-1985. Red and white were still the predominant colours in the eighties. Runners in the centre of the street waiting for the oxen to pass as they led the compact herd of Osborne bulls at full pace up the street.

8-7-1996. A sight rarely seen on Running of the Bulls photos. We see a herd of guardiolas in the lead, running full pace beneath the image of San Fermín.

In 1867, following public protests and pressure, the old route was once again adopted, this time permanently, but Chapitela had to be abandoned to be able to take in Estafeta which led to the bullring. This also came to determine even the location of the new bullring in 1922. In 1931 the way through was reduced by the Plaza del Ayuntamiento to the existing diagonal route. Successive changes to the Running of the Bulls were as a result of progressive overcrowding and its consequences, especially from towards the end of the nineteen seventies. Barricaded passages were used for the first time 1976 and in subsequent years improvements were made to the fencing and safety barriers. Estafeta is emptied

27-9-1942. In one of the Encierros *held outside the official dates, the* San Fermín chiquito, *two spectators appear to have caught the attention of a straggling bull from the* Ángel Sánchez *ranch. The fence came to be doubled as from this year. The umbrellas and raincoats explain to perfection why, four years ago, the city changed the date for the* San Fermín *celebrations from September to the first fortnight in July. The bullfight on this particular afternoon had to be suspended half way through due to the downpour.*

At the end of the fifties, a mozo running superbly in front of the bulls near the Ayuntamiento in the midst of the chaos caused by runners moving and looking in every direction.

13-7-1994. Impressive goring of a mozo by a one of the Marqués de Domecq bulls which lifted him off the ground and carried him all the way round the Plaza del Ayuntamiento or city square.

at six in the morning in order to be cleaned. The pavements have disappeared. And recently an anti-slip substance is applied in the Mercaderes area and particularly where it curves. Alterations to the bullring in 2005 involved lengthening a section of the barricaded passage and a slight change in its unevenness.

The actual starting time for the Running of the Bulls has varied a great deal. Until 1892 the bulls were let loose at six in the morning without prior notice and from 1918 to 1923 this even came to be as early as five in the morning. Since 1924 the time has moved on to seven in the morning and as from 1974 the start has been at eight on the dot. At this time, a rocket announces the opening of the corral gates and the release of the bulls. A second rocket announces when all the bulls have left and are already running. The third rocket signifies that the last bull has entered the bullring and a fourth marks the moment when all the bulls are finally in the bullring corrals.

The way in which The Running of the Bulls has changed reflects the terrain and the curves, the areas with the greatest accumulation of runners and the behaviour of the bulls. The bulls are fresh and have only recently left the corrals when they arrive at the hilly Cuesta de Santo Domingo stretch, with plenty of strength. With the help of the slope, the large fighting bulls go so fast that they almost trample on the bull-runners making their very short tailor made runs.

The herd is gathered a little as it makes its way through the Plaza del Ayuntamiento, where few people run towards where the start of Calle Mercaderes inconveniently narrows and curves slightly to the left, only to be met with sun in the eyes and fearless bulls. The bulls continue to hasten their way to Plaza de Mercaderes, without much field of vision. There are runners who try to take the curve with the herd behind, but generally there is a strong clash against the fence on the Mercaderes closed bend and the bulls either fall or slow down. Over the last few years, a group of runners have been waiting for this to happen to begin their run just when the bulls slowly and separately start to run again but the

1999. Two bulls at the head of the herd. Mozos running on the final stretch of the slope disperse whilst those waiting in the plaza *begin their run.*

13-7-2001. This example of slender, sharp horns on the Hnos. Gutiérrez Lorenzo bull "posing" before the cameras whilst slipping around the Mercaderes bend, surrounded by a throng of eager runners.

1921. The last year the Running of the Bulls finished in the old bullring. In Mercaderes square, a group of "elegant" mozos wearing suits, ties, white shoes and beret running in front of a compact herd with the bulls at the front.

anti-slip surface has considerably reduced the bulls falling.

Once in Estafeta, generally headed by the leading oxen and urged on by the herdsmen, the bulls start to run again, this time with the herd split up or spread out. In the first section on this uphill stretch the bulls move closer to the left wall whilst they herd back together. Mulling over nice runs. The herd, shortly before coming to the intersection with Bajada de Javier, makes its way down the middle of the street. The second stretch of the street

Above, the thirties. A procession of bulls head full on into the Mercaderes bend with nobody but the herdsman running. With a pike in one hand and a shirt in the other, the bulls were herded and guided by legendary figures such as Agustín Ustárroz and Germiniano Moncayola (herdsman for fighting bulls from the age of twelve) who became chief herdsmen for Running of the Bulls.

Centre, 11-7-1998. Numerous breeds of bulls or miuras *slip as they make their way along Mercaderes. In recent years an anti-slip product has been applied, especially on the Mercaderes bend. This has reduced the number of bulls falling but, the great mass of runners who precede them and block their view of the bend continue to provoke this state of affairs, albeit artificially for photographs and television cameras, and end up separating the herd and generating loose bulls along Estafeta.*

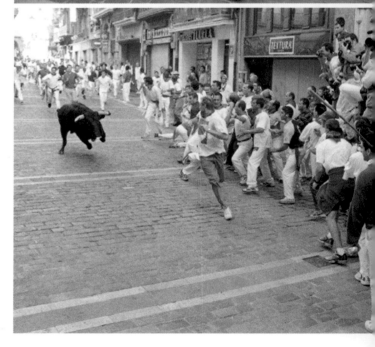

13-7-2001. One of the Hnos. Gutiérrez Lorenzo bulls "flies past" on Mercaderes after the runner in shorts.

14-7-2005. The very first Running of the Bulls for the Victorino Martín bulls in Pamplona. They very quickly and freely ran ahead of the tame bulls. Captivating sight at the top of the photograph where a victorino is clearly fixed on a runner to his right.

9-7-1955. Excellent run by one of the mozos in front of a Pablo Romero bull. Behind them, the herd moves in groups without the few runners getting too close to them.

13-7-2006. A haughty line of Fuente Ymoro bulls confidently take the bend without any problems, whilst the mozos exhibit their excellent running in front of them. Over the years difficulties have arisen on this stretch of the Encierro due to overcrowding and falling bulls.

1998. Impressive horns on the Colorado bull which, along with the rest of the herd of bulls, take the first few metres of Estafeta whilst the runners appear more attentive as to what's coming behind.

8-7-2006. Crowds of runners on a typical miuras Sunday. On the top right of the picture, a mozo is to be seen calmly leaning on a huge Miura bull as if calmly waiting for an aperitif.

straightens out and is useful for some good running, the same can be said of the Telefónica section. Complications arise again with the Running of the Bulls on the descent (sand covered until it was cobbled in 1982) down towards the narrow access passage to the bullring, the site of historic "heaps" of fallen runners. In the bullring the run becomes disrupted, the bulls (providing they aren't distracted or broken loose) follow the leading oxen or are led towards the corrals by the *dobladores*.

14-7-2003. "Pocobrío", a Sardinian bull from Torrestrella, running after the mozo in the black shirt. The bull was after him as many as three times along a 200 metre stretch on Calle Estafeta, during what was to be a very long run, with interruptions provoked by distractions and a North American whose reckless behaviour caused him to be seriously gored.

9-7-2007. Numerous bulls fall in Estafeta as the herd from Fuente Ymbro runs in a disorderly fashion. From the ground, a mozo looks helplessly at the large fighting bulls as they tower above.

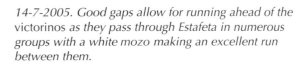

14-7-2005. Good gaps allow for running ahead of the victorinos as they pass through Estafeta in numerous groups with a white mozo making an excellent run between them.

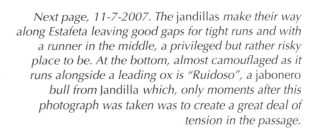

Next page, 11-7-2007. The jandillas *make their way along Estafeta leaving good gaps for tight runs and with a runner in the middle, a privileged but rather risky place to be. At the bottom, almost camouflaged as it runs alongside a leading ox is "Ruidoso", a jabonero bull from* Jandilla *which, only moments after this photograph was taken was to create a great deal of tension in the passage.*

The thirties. The bulls make their way almost individually along the final stretch of Estafeta. At this time Pamplona's best fighting bulls were the Villamarta and the Blanco (Parladé bulls).

12-7-2007. "Universal", a 575 kg Domecq bull which left a long list of gored and wounded in its path, seriously gored a young Mexican who committed the error of taking refuge in a doorway. The bull's force as it charged after two runners was such that the door was almost ripped out.

1924. A group of runners in front of the herd on the slope down to the passage around the bullring. As can be seen in the picture, this year the stalls were set up on what was originally the old bullring.

14-7-2001. An immense miura menacingly cuts across the entrance to the passage, something relatively unusual in one of these bulls. The photograph is proof in itself that, at this time, all those rounded up inside the fence leapt back, in spite of the protection from the timber.

14-7-2006. A combination of luck and skill kept this runner from suffering any greater misfortune in front of a victorino *just before reaching the passage around the bullring. This bull ran the entire course continuously thrusting its horns at the mozos.*

End of the fifties. The typical red and white attire was becoming very popular at this time. A highly risky situation at the entrance to the passage with the bull not apparently fixed on the one who has fallen.

7-7-1950. Superb profile of the Atanasio Fernández bulls as they enter the bullring behind the leading oxen. The ground surface at this time was still solid brick.

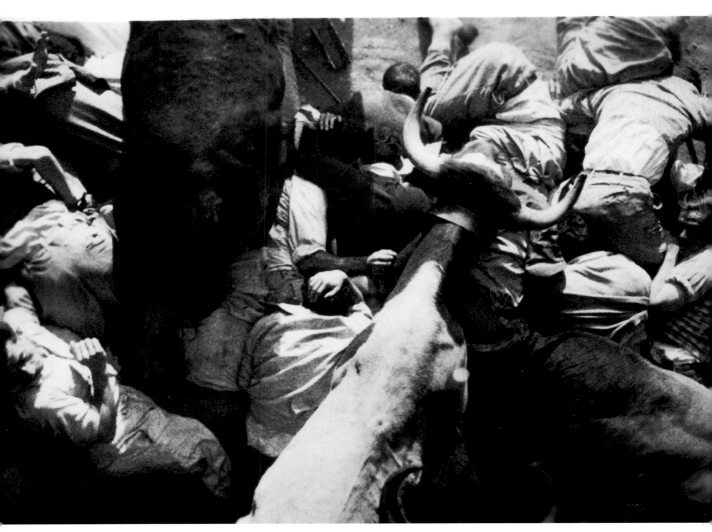

1957. Bulls and leading oxen make their way through the heap. The twenty heaps or build up of runners at the entrance to the narrow callejón or passage testifies just how dangerous is this part of the run. The greatest danger here and situations like this, is not from being gored by the bulls but by being crushed or asphyxiated.

The thirties. The runners struggle to make the end of the passage. Curious sight of a mozo with what appears to be a bag on the right of the picture. Is it possible they were churros from La Mañueta?

The fifties. The herd enters the bullring well grouped together whilst the runners disperse to prevent the beasts becoming distracted and drive them towards the corrals.

THE PRINCIPLE CHARACTERS IN THE RUNNING OF THE BULLS

THE RUNNERS

When we speak of runners we are referring to those who consciously appreciate and accept the risk of running in front of a bull and what this means. We won't go into personal reasons for taking part here, there being as many as there are

2007. To the applause of a full bullring and surrounded by the chaos of disorderly runners a mozo drives the bulls to the inside of the bullring.

Next page, end of the sixties and beginning of the seventies. Highly risky situation. The mozo appears to want to cut in front of the bull, without actually having the room to manoeuvre whilst the herdsman is running in an attempt to avoid a possible tragedy.

participants. Of course, for the locals or *los de casa* (as well as for those who come from areas on the peninsula where bullfighting is popular) the tradition is a good culture medium. Alongside these there circulates a great mass of *correteadores*, the people who are misinformed or unconsciously unaware of the real dangers. The myths and widespread media coverage have entailed progressive saturation of the stretches along the route of the Running of the Bulls making it almost impossible, for example, to see a bull coming from a distance in Calle Estafeta. Every participant has their own personal idea when it comes to preparing for the Running of the Bulls , such as a sort of calming ritual

The fifties. Good running by mozos *at the start of Mercaderes street. The red and white outfit was still a rather unusual sight at the* Encierro. *The clothing, perhaps more suited to a day at the office, helped to keep up the speed.*

repeated every day, every year. Running is something learned from questioning and listening to the veterans, and naturally also from the experience gained from bull running, year after year.

Next page, 10-7-2004. On Estafeta, a typical "bubble" or space around the bulls, in this case from the Dolores Aguirre *ranch. Amongst the front group only the white* mozo *in the centre of the picture is running in front of the bulls whilst the rest of the runners fight for a place.*

14-7-1998. At the beginning of Estafeta street, some superb running and lots of gaps before the last bull from Torrealta. From the ground, one of the Encierro's regular runners and photographer is studying the run, not clear whether he is thinking of a new composition or simply missing his camera.

12-7-2007. Four of the domecq bulls make their way along Estafeta street whilst another falls on the bend and, in the foreground, the runners take up their positions alongside the docile beasts to await the bulls. On this particular day eight runners were treated for being gored and almost a hundred were injured.

The regular runners arrive showered, after having taken a light breakfast and more or less rested. The great majority have slept some hours, something not always easy during fiestas. Some arrive with time to warm up and stretch the muscles in nearby streets and corners before joining the run. They buy the newspaper with which they will run, rolled in the same way every time although experience has shown that its use with the bull is rather limited. It serves to channel the nerves. A Running of the Bulls custom is to

7-7-2006. An instant at the Running of the Bulls. A flying runner, swept by a fallen bull as it slides along the ground. By his side, two unawares crouch down alongside the fence on almost the worst place on the Mercaderes bend. Above these, a regular at the bull running and the herdsman look towards the approaching bulls. Further into the foreground, another group of runners hope the herd will slow down on the bend so they can position themselves in front of the bulls.

unconsciously keep a tight grip throughout the run and never let go of the newspaper, not even when undergoing hospital treatment.

The usual attire is more or less the traditional black and red outfit although many add the finishing touch with a certain talisman: a green T shirt which it appears that after more than thirty years and hundreds of Running of the Bulls is perfectly reproduced every day (even the bulls are familiar with it), a semi-transparent shirt which twenty years ago was black, a fiesta neckerchief, a green cotton jacket, a white T shirt with a specific illustration, trainers specially saved all year purely for the Running of the Bulls …. amongst many others. The choice of footwear also tends to include certain trends but always with soles with a good grip. There always

End of the sixties. A solitary runner almost leads the entire herd, headed by the bulls, into the bend connecting Calle Estafeta and Telefónica, whilst the rest of the runners run alongside the bulls.

The intense look on the runners faces just minutes before the start of the Encierro, *focussed as they are on the habitual spot on Estafeta for the appearance of the herd.*

remains the odd romantic who runs in the traditional espadrilles, albeit with three layers of insoles.

The great majority of runners gather at the Cuesta de Santo Domingo and leave the Plaza del Ayuntamiento for the tourists. The hour or half-hour before the Running of the Bulls is spent with the runners chatting amongst themselves, soothing the anxieties and calming any possible nerves, cracking jokes about anything, greeting other runners, commenting on the "appearance" of the foreigners and the distracted, the passing councillor checking out the route, the megaphone announcements in various languages etc. The bull's hides appear in the press photos to identify those mistaken for being tame. The runners check the shoe laces are tied. Repeat the warm up a little. Check the watch and chat about the weather. Comment on the outcome of the Running of the Bulls from the day before.

Some of the young *mozos* who run alongside the bulls come down to join in the hymn to the Saint in the niche. Another check on the watch, another joke, warm up, or a little more stretching. The adrenaline is rising. Calculations are being made as to how many runners there will be. As the waiting time decreases, the feeling there are always too many increases.

When the watch indicates they are down to the last ten or fifteen minutes, the runners wish each other luck and disperse to take up their posts. Those who won't be running on the Santo Domingo stretch make their way slowly up the steep street and squeeze between the tourists and novices gathered in the now jam-packed Plaza del Ayuntamiento. The clock on the San Cernin tower is checked. The runner is already deep in thought in what few minutes are left. The fence is opened and each one makes their way towards their usual place, cutting through the screen made by the local police in Mercaderes, greeting the Red Cross on the other side of the fencing and the herdsmen.

Once in the habitual place for the start of the run (selected depending on personal preferences, friends, family tradition, experience…) more than one more inspection on the apparel and the shoe

8-7-1976. The guardiolas *making their way along the Mercaderes stretch. The* mozo *on the left keeps a check on his distance from the tame animal in front and the first bull. Three bulls are distracted from the run, incited by the* mozo *to their right. In the seventies, the white leading oxen or* Chopera *were unmistakable.*

The sixties. When a bull turns round, like this one in Mercaderes, it causes a scattering. The bull fixes on anything that moves. Unfortunately, nowadays, a mass of misinformed or foolhardy runners run behind the herd, apparently unaware of the risks and making the job all the more difficult for the herdsmen.

laces. A last internal hymn to the Saint. A gesture to those acquaintances running on the same stretch. Check both sides to calculate how many of the people at our side on the street can we expect to find running, which ones will be a problem, where might there finish a human heap (an accumulation of fallen runners). Last final stretch and warm up hops.

With the first rocket the pace begins to hot up. The bulls are already running. Those running on the Cuesta de Santo Domingo stretch have very little time, only metres to react, sprint and get out of the way. In the rest of the run, this rocket causes the novices, the timid and the tourists to come running out. The regular runners on these stretches don't run at this stage, they await the second rocket. Through experience they calculate the time they have left until the first sign or distant warning of the approaching bulls (flashes on the balconies, the television camera turning on a bend, the people's shouts…). At the first sign, the runner begins to make a steady run. Looking over the shoulder as we run and, at the same time, watching out for any unexpected incidents before us. Some runners deliberately advance slower at the start, still a good way from the animals. The intention is to fall behind, wait and watch out for the bulls. Those coming behind are coming increasingly faster, their speed announcing the proximity of the bulls at the head of the herd. Other runners continue to wait and finally run out like sprinters, almost level with the first bull. The sign can come in any given moment or the more or less open space announcing the animal's presence, surrounded and preceded by runners.

The *mozo* speeds up and tries to put themselves in the bull's path and run ahead or resigns to run alongside until the herd passes and then stands to one side (they must never run behind). Those who run right next to the horns know full well – with exceptions and plenty of luck- they have only a few seconds and twenty, thirty or at the most fifty metres with the bull (even less on the Cuesta de Santo Domingo). Once discomforted by the bull or motivated by the crowd the parting takes place. If the herd is well spread-out there are some who try to run with the ones to follow.

Those who fall down must remain absolutely still and protect their heads with their hands.

The *legs* always have to be saved, for energy's sake, because it's difficult to know whether the full herd has passed and because of the risk (and pleasure at the same time) of the bulls on the loose. More care has to be taken with these since these are on the alert and rise up when a runner is close or makes a gesture. Once the herd has passed, even without running behind, one never remains completely at peace and even less so on the corners and in the gateways. The shouts of the police are heard from the other side of the fence, which gives a good idea as to whether there remains any bulls on the stretch or not. Caution and experience keeps the tension running high, until the third rocket.

BULLS
The behaviour of the bulls at the Running of the Bulls has been the object of a thousand and one articles and studies but, although similar conduct has been observed in certain livestock (for example, the Cebado Gago are known to be dangerous and the Miura tend to herd together on the run), experience however shows that there are no two bulls alike and that one can never rely on labels. The specimens brought to Pamplona are noted for their great weight and good bearing and their considerable size, but the bull's behaviour amongst a herd is very different, led by oxen, surrounded and preceded by a mass of moving figures, to which the bull on the loose can turn if incited, and charge at what it believes is safe to be left still against the wall.

There are some specimens coming out of the corrals in rather a strange way and make war to get their own back, charging at everything and anything and generally spreading chaos. In 2007, the "Universal" bull from Domecq was a prime example. This bull never stopped to charge, gore, twist and turn, from Santo Domingo to the Bullring, leaving behind a long list of gored and injured. Comments have since been made that it was seen to be problematic with the rest of the herd in the Gas corrals.

12-7-2006. At the top of Calle Mercaderes, the big tame oxen placidly bringing up the rear of the Running of the Bulls.

MANSOS

Since the 1930's the bulls have been following the *mansos* or tame leading oxen from *Alaiza, Hemández, Calahorra*, de *Chopera*, etc. These are actually the most anonymous of the main contributors to the Running of the Bulls but essential for leading the herd or *enticing* difficult bulls on the loose. The first group runs with the bulls. They know the route by heart and rarely fall or stop. There are some famous specimens, almost missed by more than one runner, such as the Colorado, very quick, which for years lead at a walking pace, provoking the stampede of those who didn't want to get a close up look at a horn nor the painting and cleaning of the route for the runs. If the runner is too sure of themselves they can be seen knocked down or accidentally trampled on by the leading oxen. It is actually very rare to see them charge.

After the run, another group of oxen bring up the rear, making their way at a slow trot like a leisurely road-sweeper. There are always tourists running "terrorised" in front of these pacific creatures complete with their cowbells.

The fifties. The last of the Encierro *bulls enter the bullring tightly controlled by the herdsman. From 1947 and for many years after, the chief herdsman for the Running of the Bulls was* Teodoro Lasanta, *the chief herdsman at* Chopera, *and to whom a plaque is dedicated in the bullring's horse yard.*

HERDSMEN

In the past these were also responsible for moving the bulls on foot along the cattle tracks from the livestock farms. Nowadays they are occupied with the spirited livestock at fiestas, including that of the *Encierro*, The Running of the Bulls the *Apartado* (separating the bulls), the *Corrida* (bullfight) and the *Encierrillo* (short Running of the Bulls).

For the collective consciousness as regards the Running of the Bulls there were the legendary herdsmen such as Agustín Ustarroz from Funes and Germiniano Moncayola from Arguedas, at a time when they led the wild bulls through the streets with a staff in one hand and a shirt in the other. Present day herdsmen include José Miguel Araiz Arellano "Rastrojo", Vicente Martínez Lezano "Chichipán", Francisco Itarte and Miguel Reta, amongst others. Dressed in a green T shirt with the identifying wording on the back.

At the Running of the Bulls, the herdsmen spread out along the route and take turns, given the impossibility of doing the entire route, running after the livestock, on account of the speed and the crowds. Armed with only a staff, they lead the bulls, to avoid them turning or changing direction and help the runners in a tight spot to deal with the bull. The regular runners have great respect for the herdsmen and follow their instructions. The throngs of poor runners and the great many people who have no idea of what they have let themselves in for is a major concern for today's herdsmen, since these people touch the bulls, run after them or incite them from behind. Added to this is the desire of many to achieve momentary fame though a photograph or an instant's appearance on TV. And there are also those who seem to believe they have exclusive rights to run before the bull and have no qualms about doing so.

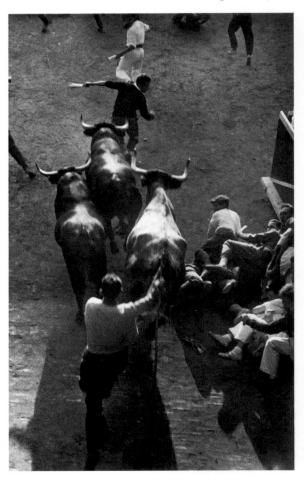

Next page, 7-7-2007. One of the Dolores Aguirre *bulls turns round, the fault being the oblivious person running behind, whilst herdsmen try to rectify the situation. In the background, visitors can be seen with T shirts taken from this year's winning poster which stated not to run behind the bulls.*

DOBLADORES

The *dobladores* came to be one of the leading participants in Running of the Bulls around 1922. We can name some very well-known *dobladores* such as Pedro Chaverri, "Chico de Olite", Julián and Isidro Marín, Jesús Gracia, Antonio Robles "El Sevilla", to which we can more recently add *dobladores* such as the Morenos, Sergio Sánchez, etc.

The majority of these come from the world of bullfighting and are former matadors, apprentice bullfighters or *banderilleros*. They are the ones in the bullring with the cape. They assist the *mozos* or bullfighter's grooms in a tight spot and lead the distracted livestock towards the corrals in the bullring. Except for extreme circumstances they aren't allowed to fight the bulls, only raise a hand to them. Their problem lies in the overcrowding, the multitudes who have no intention of running close to the bull but find themselves in the bullring, those who incite the beast or even aspire to stand out and runners who insist on running with the bulls in the sand.

8-7-1982. The doblador *raises his cape to an* Albaserrada *specimen. There were five dobladores working in Pamplona's bullring at this time: Jesús Gracia, "Sevilla", Manolo Rubio, "Romito" and Ciriaco Díez.*

7-7-2007. Taking down the fencing on the Telefónica section of the Encierro, something which has to be done by hand on a daily basis immediately the run has finished.

SAFE-CONDUCT AT THE *ENCIERRO*
FENCING OFF THE *ENCIERRO*

The fence marks out the entire route to be covered by the bulls through the city, from the Rochapea district to the Bullring. It also encloses the *Encierrillo*, the Short Bull-Run and the *Encierro* or the Running of the Bulls strictly speaking. In the past they only used to erect temporary fences around the corrals at the Casa del Toril and the bullring, both in the Plaza del Castillo, where the Running of the Bulls finished. Crossroads and street intersections were covered with blankets until the second half of the 18th century when they finally began to erect the fencing. For safety reasons, after the bulls had, on numerous occasions, broken the fence, as from 1942 the fence came to be double.

The present day fencing comes in an astonishing number of pieces, around three thousand (including planks, posts, gates, etc.), the majority in pine wood. The fencing is also marked with letters to identify the different stretches, such as A for Tejería, B for Espoz y Mina and C for Bajada de Javier. The Telefónica stretch also includes the letter R in honour of Julio Ríos, the carpenter who dealt with the fencing for half a century. During the fiestas, more than fifty carpenters (now known as *Carpintería Hermanos Aldaz Remiro*, from Puente la Reina) erect and take down the fencing on a daily basis, in an almost traditional way, to allow for the circulation.

THE RED CROSS
AND EMERGENCY SERVICES

Every day, from six in the morning, the Red Cross mobilises more than a hundred volunteers, spread out along the Running of the Bulls route in a dozen first-aid posts and four medical posts. To these we have to add the ambulances, the extra staff on at the Accident & Emergency departments in Pamplona Hospitals and the WC's conveniently located in the bullring, amongst others.

Depending on how serious and what type of injury is being attended to after the run, colour codes have been established (yellow, green and red) equally as a means of establishing the urgency of the case and arranging transport to hospital but also as a means of establishing which hospital the person is to be attended (priority is given as regards the type of injury). The ambulances, distributed alongside the Running of the Bulls route, take the injured to the hospital A & E departments in minutes.

LOCAL AND FORAL POLICE

Both forces are distributed along the various stretches of the route. They check the carpenters have erected the fences first thing. Next, a section of the route is closed (from Mercaderes to the bullring) to be cleaned. They check access is allowed to the run from 7 to 7.30 am at the authorised places. They check the route and establish screening to remove those from the run who aren't in a fit state or carry prohibited objects (rucksacks, mobile phones, cameras, bottles…..the list is almost endless). They establish police safety cordons until minutes before the run. After the first rocket is fired, they take up the gap between the fencing to prevent spectators occupying this safety zone for emergencies and which also serves as an escape for runners in need. They see to it that the injured are attended to. In the bullring, where thousands of people gather at the sound of the first rocket, a great while before the last bull leaves the Santo Domingo corral, the Foral police have the task of trying to keep crowds out of the access passage and to ensure there are empty spaces behind the barrier, the *burladeros* (wooden boards the bullfighters stand behind) and the bullring passage.

Next page, 1945. The police attempt to hold back the mass of runners on the fencing barrier by the Pirineo bar. Years later, on 7-7-1960, a similar scene whereby the police overdid the opening in the fence on the sloping Bajada de Javier stretch provoking a historical montón *or pile up at this point on Estafeta. Those who went by shortly after on this 1960* Encierro *testified to their being virtually a sea of abandoned shoes.*

1905. The Mayor of Pamplona, Joaquín Viñas, seen here on Espoz y Mina (street now named Duque de Ahumada) as he takes what was the very first morning walk prior to the Encierro *run. As from this year the walk became an established tradition.*

MEMORIES AND APPETITE
PHOTOGRAPHS AND AUDIOVISUAL PRESENTATIONS

Alongside the hundreds of onlookers and locals who positively immortalise the Running of the Bulls from their streets and balconies, there are also professional photographers for the Running of the Bulls. For the type of work they do (especially those who work from the fence itself) and their special relation with the runners, these too play an important role in the Running of the Bulls (the photography shops, the media, etc). We mention but a few, such as the now deceased Javier Retegui Zubieta, Jose Luis Leache, Pío Guerendiain, Mena, Arturo, Bozano, Galle, Gómez, Calleja, Auma, Larrión and Pimoulier, etc. The photographs of the Running of the Bulls, displayed on a daily basis by the photograph shops, whether in the shop windows or on the great photograph display boards, are quite spectacular.

Whether for good or bad, the audiovisual presentations have now definitively recognised The Running of the Bulls as a universal icon. By radio, TV or Internet, every morning literally millions of people follow the bulls and *mozos* as they run through the streets of Pamplona.

Breakfasts, almuerzos and *churros*

In a city renowned for its love of good food, the breakfast and mid-morning *almuerzo de Encierro* just have to be preordained traditions. The runners usually prefer to leave the main part of the *almuerzo* until after the run. And the spectators' early rise to get a place also tends to awaken the appetite.

A typical sight on San Fermín mornings, crowds looking at photographs of bulls and runners in shop windows and on boards only a short time after the Encierro has finished.

15-12-2007. La Mañueta, the indispensable churrería celebrates 135 years of uninterrupted business. In the picture, the curious "gastronomic" necklace hanging on one of the Mañueta street giants, built by the grandfather and founder of the aforementioned churreria.

After the *Encierro* there comes a change. Some opt to join the queue for the delicious and unequalled *churros* (fried sugar coated sticks of dough) from the *"La Mañueta" churrería* (with more than 135 years in existence and still using traditional methods and equipment and wood which has been chopped by hand). Others opt for a good drinking chocolate with *churros* to dip. And more than one opts for the rather more convincing alternative, a plate with a couple of fried eggs and pork slices, to which is then added two types of sausage *txistorra* and *chorizo*, fried potatoes, tomato sauce and *ajoarriero*, a salt cod stew, and whatever else there might be. All washed down in true local style.

The city's traditional patisseries are another excellent choice for sweetening the palate, as can be seen by these truffles and chocolate specialities from Pastas Beatriz.

If these window blinds weren't lowered during the Running of the bulls, even the bulls wouldn't be able to resist the aroma from Pastis Beatriz, the patisserie in the middle of Calle Estafeta.

A traditional San Fermín almuerzo *or breakfast cum lunch in the Plaza del Ayuntamiento, next to the now demolished Casa Casla. Also present at the banquet are bearded* Kiliki *and* Zaldiko, *taken from the city's collection of Giants and Big-Heads.*

We would like to thank the following for their co-operation and their assistance in gathering the essential photographic material for this book, Mr. Javier Bergua (Colecciones Iruña) and Mr. Carlos Leandro, and for the photographs, Mr. José Ángel Ayerra Bastero, Mr. César Eugui Gauna, Mr. Miguel Lacunza Ayerra, Mr. José Luis Leache (Foto Leache), Foto Mena, Mr. Fermín Muñoz Monllor, Postales Iruña, the family of Mr. Javier Retegui Zubieta, and Mr. José Carlos Ronda Sáez from Lafuente, who we must thank for having made the book possible. In the same way we would also like to thank postcard publishers García Garrabella (Foto Chapresto) from Zaragoza and Postales Vaquero from Pamplona. Where it has not been possible to identify the persons responsible, the material is shown under the name of Mr. Carmelo Butini